Overwhelmed:

Biblical & practical ways to manage a crazy-busy homeschool life

By Terrie Bentley McKee

Overwhelmed

Overwhelmed

Overwhelmed: Biblical & practical ways to manage

a crazy-busy homeschool life

Copyright © 2022 by Terrie Bentley McKee ALL RIGHTS

RESERVED

Unless otherwise indicated, all Scripture references are

from the English Standard Version

Homeschooling1Child.com – blog by Terrie McKee

ISBN: 978-0-578-37605-9

Proudly printed in the United States of America

Overwhelmed

Overwhelmed

Dedicated to the glory of God through His
Son, Jesus Christ

In memory of my mother,
Martha Breneman Bentley

Many thanks to the following:
My husband, Greg
My son, Sam
My son and daughter-in-love, Jacob and
Allyssa
My daughter and son-in-love, Elli and Justin
My daughter, Laura
My neighbors, David, Jean, and Tobias

And special thanks to my friend Durenda
Wilson, who encourages so many
homeschooling families, including mine

Overwhelmed

Overwhelmed

Chapter One

Overwhelmed

Do you ever feel like if *one more thing* happens, you just cannot take it anymore? You'll do something drastic, like throw clothes off a balcony, or scream into the dead of night, waking up all the suburbanites. I once got so frustrated because I felt like I wasn't being heard that I grabbed a dirty pot out of the sink, ran outside, and beat that pot against a porch railing until it was horribly misshapen and unusable. Poor pot didn't see it coming.

Overwhelmed

I did feel better, for a time.

We live in an age where information is at our fingertips, and we are just inundated with stuff: trivia, answers, noise, questions…the noise infiltrates our minds, and we cannot sleep at night. Before streaming services were a thing, when a television show's season ended, we (in the olden days) had *reruns*. Television networks would play a whole season of shows over the summer—they would run them again; therefore, reruns. Now, we can binge-watch at will. In the dead of night, as you try to sleep, you play the reruns of the day in your

Overwhelmed

head: should I have said that? Why didn't I do that? Is that project done?

We worry-pray for each of our children and wonder if we were good enough in whatever pursuit we hunted that day.

In short, we are overwhelmed. I remember a trip to Philadelphia once, with my then-boyfriend. I had my two boys and he had his daughter, and we went to Philly to visit his parents (and, unbeknownst to me, get engaged). While in Philly, we visited the busy Reading Market: a cornucopia of foods, sights, sounds, and smells. Greg, who likes such things, likened it to a flea market of food. I don't care for flea markets, so I

Overwhelmed

was positively overwhelmed with the sensory overload. In fact, I got lost, so I sat down on the floor at the base of a column and called him on his phone, crying. He came over to where I was, huddled on the floor, reached down, and walked me back to the table, his arm around me.

Being overwhelmed with life is nothing new, but man! There isn't much that can destroy one's productivity or jeopardize one's confidence more than being overwhelmed. There are so many things that can overwhelm us: crushing schedules, sour relationships, paralyzing grief, powerlessness, endless to-do lists, chronic

Overwhelmed

pain and illness, and—hold on—*high expectations.*

We look at some Christian homeschoolers and think, *they've got it all figured out.* Nice home, well-behaved children, steady and good income with money in savings. *God has certainly blessed them.* Friend, you can have a nice home, well-behaved children, and money, and still be far off from God. None of that makes you a Christian, only Jesus. We tend to look at other Christians for inspiration and encouragement instead of looking to the One who can do something about it. Yes, Jesus.

Overwhelmed

As homeschoolers, our lives are turned up a notch: we not only have the normal crazy, but we also choose to have school in our homes, too. The operative word is "choose." If you come by homeschooling intentionally or by accident, we still choose to homeschool. Every aspect of our lives revolves around our children and their education: how they learn, what their interests are, and the best curriculum to foster those interests.

The overwhelmed part happens when we look at other homeschooling parents and compare our lives with theirs, or when life with all its ups-and-downs overtake us, or

Overwhelmed

when our expectations don't mesh with reality.

Our God is God of order, not chaos. When our homeschools dovetail with God's will (and not the other way around), we stand a much better chance of containing the crazy and not getting overwhelmed.

We look at our Bibles and think, "Everyone in the Bible had it going on. No issues. They knew just what to do." Hogwash and burnt toast. *Everyone* in the Bible was overwhelmed at one time or another. We are going to dive in and see how our forefathers and foremothers of faith handled stress, anxiety, being overwhelmed…and take away some incredibly valuable tips and tools to manage this crazy-busy life we live—as homeschoolers.

Action Items

1. What are your expectations for your homeschool?
2. Are there things in your life that you can give up for this busy season you're in? What are they?
3. Think about people in the Bible. Which ones can you think of that were under immense stress?

Bible Verses

Write these out in the space given:

Philippians 4:6-7

Psalm 46:1

Overwhelmed

Romans 8:28

Philippians 4:8

Psalm 94:19

Jeremiah 17:7-8

Chapter Two

Besor Moments

The Amalekites were relentless enemies of Israel and Judah in the time of David. They invaded the south and attacked Ziklag, a provincial town located in the Negev, in Judah. First Samuel 30:2 states that the Amalekites burned Ziklag to the ground "and had taken captive the women and those who were there, from small to great; they did not kill anyone, but carried them away and went their way." When David and his army came to Ziklag, they found it burning, but all the children and the women,

Overwhelmed

including David's wives Ahinoam and Abigail, had been taken captive.

Overwhelmed, distraught with grief, David and his army "lifted up their voices and wept, until they had no more power to weep," [v. 4].

When my husband, Greg, was shot and paralyzed in an attempted armed robbery, I was beside myself with shock and grief. At the rest area where the shooting took place, I screamed and cried out, shaking uncontrollably. My body went into fight-or-flight mode, and finding nothing to fight and nowhere to flee, it shook and shrieked. When we come face-to-face with trauma or

Overwhelmed

overwhelming powerlessness, we lift up our voices and weep. The word "weep" is often misunderstood as it sounds, quite frankly, like a meek little word. One imagines Southern debs with pristine, starched handkerchiefs dabbing at the corners of their eyes. But really, it means to sob, cry out, wail…. It does not mean to sniffle, blow your nose, and go about your day.

David and his men *wept* and when the men had finally met their senses halfway, they turned their grief into anger towards David. Verse six is powerful because it is indicative of two ways of dealing with this kind of overwhelming grief: "Now David

Overwhelmed

was greatly distressed, for the people spoke of stoning him, because the soul of all the people was grieved, every man for his sons and his daughters. But David strengthened himself in the LORD his God."

Then men, overcome with grief, focused their pain on their leader and decided he must die. But look at what David did: he *strengthened himself in the LORD his God."* We can either allow being overwhelmed to take us on a self-destructive path, or we can lift our eyes to our Lord. Philippians 4:12-13 states, "I know how to be abased, and I know how to abound. Everywhere and in all things I have learned both to be full and to be hungry, both to abound and to suffer need. I can do all things through Christ who strengthens me."

Most people quote Philippians 4:13 but I believe it has more meaning with verse 12. We can be full or hungry, have nothing or have everything, but to have the kind of mindset where we can be content in all those things, and deal with whatever life throws at us, we need the strength that Christ provides. David lifted his eyes to the Lord, and what happened? *He was strengthened.*

When we focus on the things around us that are overwhelming, like the Reading Market, all we see are the stands upon

Overwhelmed

stands of people selling all sorts of food with smells that invade our nostrils. We twirl around in the mad dash of people buying spices or beefsteak sandwiches or even baba ganoush. It's only when we get still, that we can look up at our Savior reaching down for us and leading us to His rest.

When we start the day late—getting up way later than we should, or not spending the time in the morning easing into the day putting God first, we tend to bark at the kids and get their day started off rough, too. I'm writing to the choir here. Before David started running toward the kidnappers, he consulted the Lord.

Overwhelmed

As homeschoolers, we need to go before the Lord to learn from Him before we try to teach our own children. We cannot fill our children's cups if we're attempting to pour into them from an empty cup. Cups can only be filled by Christ.

David did something else, though. Even though the stoning was abated, he still had an overwhelming problem: the Amalekites had invaded his territory and had kidnapped women and children. He did not scream out, "Charge!" with swords flashing and horses rearing in anticipation. Scripture tells us that "…David said to Abiathar the priest, Ahimelech's son, 'Please bring the ephod

Overwhelmed

here to me.' And Abiathar brought the ephod to David. So David inquired of the LORD, saying, 'Shall I pursue this troop? Shall I overtake them?'" [verses 7-8a].

David *prayed*. He inquired of the Lord what his next move should be. He didn't fly off the handle and attack without the Lord's blessing. I have personally experienced the most glorious defeats when I *reacted* to being overwhelmed, charging headlong into my will, instead of being in the Presence of the Lord and asking *Him* about *His* will, and His direction.

Overwhelmed

The Lord answered: "Pursue, for you shall surely overtake them and without fail recover all." [verse 8b].

The next half of this story is so touching to my heart. The men, under David, set out to overtake the Amalekites, and eventually they came to the brook Besor. Six hundred men and David stopped at the brook Besor, but two hundred of his men were too weary and faint to continue. David told them to rest while he and the four hundred remaining carried on.

This is important. There is no shame in saying you cannot go on another step, that you are too weary with grief, fatigue, or the

Overwhelmed

busyness of life. There is no shame to say you need a break from homeschooling and take a week off. Psalm 23:2-3a states that the Lord "makes me to lie down in green pastures; He leads me beside the still waters. He restores my soul…" Besor was known for being a large, yet peaceful oasis in the uninhabitable Negev. Surrounded by palm trees and lush grasses, it was the perfect remedy for the weary soldiers so full of grief. When we notice friends or family members nearly done in by troubles, we need to step up, and get them to rest while we handle things. If we are the ones overwhelmed with life or troubles, we need to openly call up a friend or family member

Overwhelmed

and tell them I need a "Besor moment."
There is no shame in resting, dear heart.

This same peaceful brook was very wide and here the men were, emotionally done, physically tired, worried beyond belief—and now they had to cross this huge stretch of water. It was too much. They came to the end of the rope and had to sit down. Already overwhelmed with losing their wives and children, walking through a wide body of water was just too much.

Have you ever had a "Besor moment?" Your day is already bad, it's taken a turn for the worse, and now it's raining while you're driving, the kids are fighting…you just want

Overwhelmed

to go home, order a pizza delivery, and get in your pajamas. You just cannot deal with one more thing—but here's someone calling you out on something you did or didn't do, and it just adds to your anxiety. The Israelite soldiers dealt with that, too.

When the four hundred came back, having been victorious over the Amalekites and retrieved their families, there was talk about not sharing the spoils with the two hundred who had stayed behind. But David called them out on that, saying, "My brethren, you shall not do so with what the LORD has given us, who has preserved us and delivered into our hand the troop that

Overwhelmed

came against us. For who will heed you in this matter? But as his part is who goes down to the battle, so shall his part be who stays by the supplies; they shall share alike." [verses 23-24].

Instead of being like the Israelite soldiers that went to battle, we need to look out for others. Do you see a friend post on social media that they're overwhelmed and just cannot do it any more today? Instead of offering advice or saying they did it to themselves, just be like Jesus: bring a meal over. Come in with pizza, Chinese, or other take-out, and offer to fold some laundry. Hold the baby so Mom can get a shower.

Overwhelmed

You know, life is so hard—and we need to reach out to those who are overwhelmed to the point of tears and give them a hand.

Listen: homeschool is hard enough, and we all need encouragement. If you see a homeschool parent struggling with some sort of issue, why not lend a hand? Offer to bring a casserole over, or cut the grass? These "Besor moments" can be thought of in this social media world as a cry for help, a "I just can't even," or "I give up." If you see a parent with such a status or if they say something like that at a playdate, they need help—whether or not they homeschool.

Overwhelmed

It's one thing to tell someone you're praying for them. It's a good thing, prayer. But prayer with love-in-action is something else. If someone says to you, "I am so tired and I'm not feeling well…" telling them you're praying for them is okay. But telling them, "Hey, I'm bringing you a meal so you don't have to cook tonight," and offering a prayer *with* your friend while presenting a casserole or take-out—that's love-in-action. Jesus just didn't tell a hungry crowd that He'd pray for them; He fed them.

Be the kind of Christian to others that you'd want for yourself. "Do to others as

Overwhelmed

you would have them do to you," said Jesus [Luke 6:31].

Conversely, it's awfully easy for those who are overwhelmed to isolate themselves from others. Often it is a coping mechanism. Sometimes life gets so hard that you feel as though you must circle the wagons and stop doing a lot of things with friends, family— even going to church can seem like a big deal, and honestly, it can be. When my family and I go to church, what with my husband needing a handicapped parking place since he's in a wheelchair, it can be just plain hard if all the handicapped spots are taken and he has to park elsewhere. It

Overwhelmed

makes a hard situation that much more difficult. If you notice people not being as active as they once were, call them up and ask if they're okay. Better yet, invite them over for a meal and fellowship.

Everyone has a story. Everyone gets overwhelmed at times, and we all need a break now and then. We need to be on the lookout for people who are overwhelmed, at the end of their ropes, so we can help them. The Body of Christ exists to be the family of Jesus on Earth, to help each other. When we do that, it becomes a testimony and a witness to those who don't yet know Jesus.

Action Items

1. Make and freeze a few casserole dishes in disposable containers with lids, making sure you write the reheating instructions and name of the dish on the lid. Put in the freezer for anyone who may need a meal—or your own family, for those crazy-busy days.
2. Buy some "thinking of you" cards, restaurant gift cards, and stamps. When you hear of someone struggling, send them a note of encouragement and a gift card. It doesn't have to be a lot—even a $10 coffee gift card will tell a parent that you're thinking of them.
3. If you're struggling, be sure to tell someone who will care and do something about it. Work on nurturing a tribe around you who will take care of one another.

Bible Verses

Write these out in the space given:

John 15:12-13

Overwhelmed

1 Peter 4:8

1 Corinthians 16:13-14

Galatians 6:2

Hebrews 13:16

Chapter Three

Special Needs

When I was a young girl, I had a speech impediment in which I would reverse the sounds of *r* and *w*. You know, *rabbit* became *wabbit* and *great* became *gweat*. I was embarrassed and went through years of speech therapy.

Finally, I learned that if I growl out the *r* sound, it would come out like *grrreat* and *rrrabbit*. To this day, when I'm talking fast or not intentionally, I struggle with reversing those letter sounds. So, when I'm speaking

Overwhelmed

to a group, I tend to talk slowly and highly intentionally. Unfortunately, the slower I talk, the more my Southern drawl comes out. It's a vicious cycle.

When God called Moses into service, one of Moses' chief excuses was that he had a speech impediment. Moses said in Exodus 4:10 (ESV), "But Moses said to the LORD, "Oh, my Lord, I am not eloquent, either in the past or since you have spoken to your servant, but I am slow of speech and of tongue."

We all have issues that we were born with that slow us down, embarrass us, and quite frankly, overwhelm us in certain

Overwhelmed

situations. For years and years, I grappled with the idea of public speaking – or even standing before my classmates and reciting a poem. The thought of doing that and reversing all my *r's and w's* was too much to bear, and often I willingly took a failing grade that to recite something. It's overwhelming.

In high school, we had to stand before the entire class and recite Shakespeare's "To Be or Not To Be" soliloquy from *Hamlet*. When I stood at the front, all eyes on me, I completely forgot it. So, I said, "To be—or not to be—and that's all I have to say about that." I sat down quickly and noticed many

Overwhelmed

mouths were agape, wide open, including my teacher's—but some heads were nodding. They got it. They understood. I very willingly took the failing grade.

Moses was overwhelmed with his speech impediment, too. But God was not having it: He had chosen Moses to be His spokesperson before Pharoah, and He knew what He was doing. He told Moses in verse 11, "Who has made man's mouth? Who makes him mute, or deaf, or seeing, or blind? Is it not I, the LORD? Now therefore go, and I will be with your mouth and teach you what you shall speak."

Overwhelmed

As a mom of a child (adult child, but my child nonetheless) who has autism, I understand Moses' dilemma. Conversely, I find God's answer interesting. *Who makes him mute, or deaf, or seeing, or blind?*

This tells me that despite our disabilities or excuses, God has a plan and a purpose—and can use us for His plan and purpose. We often ask God, "Why?" Why is my son autistic? Why do I have rheumatoid arthritis? Why is my husband paralyzed? *Why why why?*

Yet, there's God in the background, saying to us, "Don't you think I know this? Don't you think I can use this to my glory?

Overwhelmed

Don't you think I love you and want to involve you in my kingdom work—despite, because, and through your disabilities?"

God often uses these situations to fulfil His promise to Moses that He would "be with your mouth and teach you what you shall speak," but for us. Luke 12:12 states that "…the Holy Spirit will teach you in that very hour what you ought to say." So when it's time to advocate for your child, stand up for your right to homeschool, or work through a tough conversation with your children, trust that with prayer, God will give you the words to say.

Overwhelmed

It comes down to a matter of *trust*. Trusting God in our seasons of being overwhelmed that *He sees us, He knows us, and He hears us*. He knows we're overwhelmed because of *fill-in-the-blank*. Having children with disabilities, I have found, means being overwhelmed *and* lonely. How comforting it is to know that Jesus sees, hears, and knows us!

When Sam was younger and he'd throw ungodly tantrums in stores, yes, it was embarrassing. When he was a young boy and would never sleep through the night, and have screaming fits at two in the morning, all because of autism, it was

Overwhelmed

overwhelming. I was going to school full-time, working part-time, in a terrible marriage in which the dad would hardly ever help, and dealing with this toddler…it was catastrophically overwhelming to my sleep-deprived body.

Yet, God…Jesus saw my desperate state and I turned, after years of seeing it collect dust, to my Bible. I started reading the Word and trusting in Christ and seeing that He had a plan for my son, though I couldn't see it.

Going back to Moses, it's interesting that he haggles with God, saying, "Oh, my Lord, please send someone else," (verse 13). When God calls *you* to be the parent of a special needs child, He's calling *you*. He doesn't have someone else in mind. When God calls *you* to go through trials and tribulations, building a testimony that will shine the Gospel into dark places, He's not calling someone else. He's using the calling and the testimony He's investing in *you* to share the Gospel.

When I went on a group mission trip to Zambia, Africa in 2013, we were told that a large percentage of women are in abusive marriages there. Wife-beating is a normal occurrence. Having escaped an abusive marriage in 2005, I understood, all too well, the overwhelming desperation the Zambian

Overwhelmed

women faced. One night, we were visiting houses in the village in which orphans (usually from AIDS) lived, six to a house, with an unrelated "house mother" who took care of them. The particular house with whom I was to visit had a mother who served only on the weekends, to give the weekly house mother a break, to go home to her own family.

After I shared the Gospel with the six children, leading four of them to Christ, the house mother asked me to come to her bedroom. She shared with me her story: during the week she lived at her home, only to be beaten and raped by her alcoholic

Overwhelmed

husband. She was ashamed and felt dirty.

Tears dripping off my face, I shared with her

my testimony of my abusive, alcoholic

husband who I had left eight years prior. I

told her God redeemed that, and He could

redeem her, too. Jesus used my testimony

that He built and led this sweet young

woman to Himself.

> "Blessed be the God and Father of our Lord Jesus Christ, the Father of mercies and God of all comfort, *who comforts us in all our affliction*, so that *we* may be able to *comfort those who are in any affliction*, with the comfort with which we ourselves are comforted by God. For as we share abundantly in Christ's sufferings, so through Christ we share abundantly in

Overwhelmed

> comfort too. If we are afflicted, it is for your comfort and salvation; and if we are comforted, it is for your comfort, which you experience when you patiently endure the same sufferings that we suffer." [2 Corinthians 1:3-6 emphasis mine]

You see, God comforts us in all our afflictions, so that we may be able to comfort others, and share the Gospel with them, *because of the testimony He gives us*.

Moses was embarrassed and overwhelmed with the task God was asking him to do: be God's mouthpiece to Pharoah. When Moses said to find someone else, God became angry, and decided maybe His mouthpiece needed a mouthpiece. Moses wasn't going to get off that easily. God had planned Moses' path for him before his mother placed him in the basket in the waters, and if he had to have a one-on-one helper to do it, so be it.

God enlisted Moses' brother Aaron to speak for him, and set them off to Egypt to tell Pharoah, "let My people go!" Eventually, Moses found his own voice, and despite being overwhelmed by his speech, he followed God's plan for his life and led the Israelites out of bondage.

David and Mephibosheth

David's best friend was Jonathan, the son of Saul, David's on-again/off-again

Overwhelmed

mortal enemy. Some time after Saul and Jonathan were killed in battle and David became king, David asked if there were any members of Saul's family who he could show "God's kindness," [2 Samuel 9:3].

Saul's servant, Ziba, told David about Jonathan's son, Mephibosheth, who was lame in both feet. He became disabled when he was five years old, when "…his nurse took him up and fled, and as she fled in her haste, he fell and became lame," [2 Samuel 4:4 NIV].

In those days, being disabled meant a terrible life of begging for food, being mistreated and alienated, and being told the condition was a punishment from God. In fact, the name "Mephibosheth" in Hebrew means "from the mouth of shame[1]."

Yet, David in "God's kindness," extended the love and friendship he had for Jonathan to Mephibosheth. When Mephibosheth came, David greeted him warmly—not because of his disability, but because of *who he was*. "And Mephibosheth the son of Jonathan, son of Saul, came to David and fell on his face and paid homage. And David said, "Mephibosheth!" And he answered, "Behold, I am your servant," [2 Samuel 9:6].

Overwhelmed

As a mom of special needs children and the wife of a man who is a full-time wheelchair user, it is critically important that we see the *person* first, not the disability. Yes, we homeschool based on our child's abilities, but like David, we see *the child* first. I love that David's exclamation of "Mephibosheth!" seemed like he was excited to see him. Be encouraged—God sees you as you struggle to do what is right for your child with special needs and on days when it's difficult. Fear can take hold that we're inadequate (hint: most homeschooling parents feel inadequate more than not) and can't homeschool our children who have special needs or have serious

Overwhelmed

medical issues, but God sees all that and will give us the strength to do what we can for our children.

God loves your children even more than you do. "And David said to him, "Do not fear, for I will show you kindness for the sake of your father Jonathan, and I will restore to you all the land of Saul your father, and you shall eat at my table always," [2 Samuel 9:7]. Even though David had just given Mephibosheth a grand estate and therefore an income, he did more than that: he gave him a seat for life at the king's table, though Mephibosheth was lame and by the world's standards, useless, doomed to be alone for the rest of his life. Because of Mephibosheth's relationship with Jonathan, King David gave him a lifelong seat at his glorious table.

It is because of our relationship with Jesus, despite our weaknesses and shortcomings, that God writes our names in the Book of Life and allows us a seat at *His table* for all eternity.

When we think of disabled people in the Bible, we often think of the people whom Jesus healed. Yet, Isaac was blind, Jacob limped, Moses stuttered, Ehud's right hand was shriveled, and Samson, the strongest man in the Bible, died blind with a limp.

Overwhelmed

God didn't shirk away from using people who had disabilities. Take heart! He can use you and your child—despite, because, and through—any disabilities you face as a family.

Holding back

We all have things in our lives that are holding us back, and sometimes those things overwhelm us to the point of being paralyzed in fear of failure. I mentioned about my own speech issues and fearing speaking in front of classmates. Ironically, due to constantly having to speak to people about my autistic son's needs in schools and therapists, I eventually learned to conquer my fear of public speaking. With the Lord's

Overwhelmed

help, I now speak in front of hundreds of people—even if I do manage to reverse *r's* and *w's* on occasion.

I know how hard and emotional it can be to homeschool and/or parent a child with special needs—especially a complicated, multi-faceted disability such as my son Sam, who has autism, bipolar disorder, epilepsy, ADHD, and intellectual disability. I know, though, that the God of the mountains is the very same God of the valleys, and *you can homeschool your child with special needs*, with the Lord's help.

There are so many parents who are homeschooling children who have special

Overwhelmed

needs, and these parents are a storehouse of information, tips, information, and help. Homeschool conventions or online homeschooling conferences often feature sessions on homeschooling special needs children, so I would encourage you to search these out and participate. They're a wealth of information so that you can learn how not to re-create the wheel.

Everyone has something that they're going through that overwhelms them: perhaps it's a special needs relative, or a disability, or an annoyance like my speech impediment. You may have a child who has

Overwhelmed

a disability or disorder that can be overwhelming at times.

We need to see God's hand in these things as part of His plan to encourage others despite, because, and through our own troubles, and use them as part of our testimonies. After all, that's why God gave them to us.

Action Items

1. If you have a child with special needs, think back throughout the past and take note of God's hand in your child's life. Pray prayers of gratitude for those things.
2. Try to find someone who would watch your child for you for an afternoon, a day, or even an overnight, just to get some respite. Research camps for your child's particular diagnosis and sign them

up. I did this for my son and it was great for him and for us.
3. If you have a child with special needs and other children who don't have diagnoses, be sure to spend one-on-one time with them. Siblings of children with special needs often feel overlooked, with all the care that the special needs child requires.

Bible Verses

Write these out in the space given:

John 9:2-4

Psalm 139:13-14

Overwhelmed

Deuteronomy 27:18-19

Leviticus 19:14

Chapter Four

Control

One of my most favorite Bible stories is a little-known one, but it encapsulates a lot about my overwhelmed life in just seven short verses – but what lessons are to be learned in those seven verses!

> "Now the sons of the prophets said to Elisha, "See, the place where we dwell under your charge is too small for us. Let us go to the Jordan and each of us get there a log, and let us make a place for us to dwell there." And he answered, "Go." Then one of them said, "Be pleased to go with your servants." And he answered,

Overwhelmed

> "I will go." So he went with them. And when they came to the Jordan, they cut down trees. But as one was felling a log, his axe head fell into the water, and he cried out, "Alas, my master! It was borrowed." Then the man of God said, "Where did it fall?" When he showed him the place, he cut off a stick and threw it in there and made the iron float. And he said, "Take it up." So he reached out his hand and took it." [2 Kings 6:1-7]

As the servant was using a borrowed axe to fell a tree to build a shelter near the mighty Jordan River, his axe head fell off and sank into the water. Can't you just hear the desperation of his voice as he said, "It was *borrowed!*"

Overwhelmed

Oh my, how many times have we been in this situation? Someone brings over a casserole in a time of need, but they don't bring it in a disposable foil container; they bring it in their best glass casserole dish. You know the one, with the fancy plastic lid that fits oh-so-securely. You eat and enjoy the casserole, but in the process of cleaning it, it falls off the drying towel that's on the countertop and plummets to the floor. How do you explain this to your friend? You're embarrassed and you're out the money to replace it, lid and all.

Here's this servant using an axe that was borrowed, and he lost the iron axe head in

Overwhelmed

the powerful Jordan River, which is deep in places and this was obviously one of those places. He can't find it; this is one of those times in the Bible that "freaking out" is Scriptural.

I've been there so many times. How many times do I lose my keys and therefore my mind, getting more frantic by the moment? Or I lose a truly important piece of paper and cannot find it anywhere – dreading that I may have accidentally thrown it away. Once I threw away something important, totally by accident, and combed through the trash in the

Overwhelmed

household dumpster until it was found. I washed my hands fourteen times!

I once bought an expensive, albeit used spiral bound workbook that was part of a science curriculum for my daughter. I took it home and start planning for the new year, only to find it had been marked in by a *much younger* child. I could just hear that mom: "But I was going to sell it!" Here's a tip: always look *through* used workbooks before purchasing!

When my youngest son was just a little boy, he had a beloved stuffed bear named, oddly enough, "Baby Bear." We were in a large discount store and he was in the cart,

Overwhelmed

throwing Baby Bear in the air and catching him. He did this several times as I zipped along, hurrying to get my shopping done to go home and cook dinner.

Suddenly, Jacob began to howl and scream and cry. He yelled, "Baby Bear's *gone!*"

We looked and looked all over. Did he drop Baby Bear? He didn't know. His little four-year old self couldn't remember where we were when Baby Bear disappeared, but disappeared he had.

We left; what else could we do? We went home, Jacob crying the whole way, and I made dinner. He refused to eat – which

Overwhelmed

made me think this was serious. For the boy to refuse food was unheard-of. I bathed him and put him to bed, and he asked if we could pray. Of course we could pray!

A week passed. Seven days of nightly praying and crying for Baby Bear. Finally, I went back to the discount store by myself and I prayed and prayed. Suddenly, overcome by the Holy Spirit, I was moved to go to the spaghetti sauce aisle. I reached up on the top shelf, past the marinara and pesto…*Baby Bear!* I yelled, "Praise YOU Jesus!" A large woman pushing a cart towards me yelled out, "Yes! Praise Jesus! Praise HIM!" She had no idea why the

Overwhelmed

spontaneous praise session was happening, but it didn't matter. My son was overjoyed that Baby Bear was found, but more importantly—he learned an important lesson about prayer. There is nothing too small for God to be concerned about, and nothing too big He cannot do.

We tend to go about our planning and curriculum-buying without much input from God, but expect Him to bless it. God is interested in our prayers, no matter how small or insignificant they seem to be to us—even about curriculum or co-op or other homeschooling choices. If God can take pity on a servant's frantic prayer over a sunken axe-head, don't you think He cares about the curriculum you are considering for your homeschool?

These children He has given you to rear in His name, He loves them more than you do. Truly. He cares about their education, their welfare, their health—and their souls, more than anything. Jesus *loves* children—and He loves *your child*.

In the iron axe-head story, God bent His own laws of physics to take a heavy, dense, iron tool to make it float to the top. Certainly, a miracle occurred that day that turned those men's hearts to God. There is nothing God cannot do to turn hearts to

Overwhelmed

Him. It may be painful, it may not be what we expect or anticipate—but if we trust Him and are in the center of His will, there is no need to fear or be overwhelmed with things that aren't in our control (as if anything is truly in our control).

Friend, take heart: Jesus sees you. He sees the work you pour into your children, wondering if it will stick like so much done spaghetti thrown on the wall. He hears your prayers, wondering if you're choosing the right resources or therapies. Faith in Jesus is not an untouchable thing, way up in the sky—it's right there with you on the sofa as you read to your child, patiently moving a

Overwhelmed

finger from word to word as you enunciate, praying silently within your heart and mind that it's taking root.

Jesus will take whatever you drop, when you pray and have faith, and return it to you, if it's His will to do so. Everything asked of Jesus must be in keeping with His Holy Will. We falter when we don't realize this, and then spin our spiritual wheels turning and trying to fix things ourselves. That breeds an overwhelming, frustrating spirit.

People sometimes say, "God won't put on you anymore than you can handle." This is false, a twisting of Scripture by satan himself. The actual verse is 1 Corinthians

Overwhelmed

10:13 (ESV): "No temptation has overtaken you that is not common to man. God is faithful, and He will not let you be tempted beyond your ability, but with the temptation He will also provide the way of escape, that you may be able to endure it." It is talking about *temptation*, not overwhelming situations. In those overwhelming times, we must not think we can handle them by ourselves; we need to turn to God because He *is* faithful and *will* be with you in these times because He *promised* He would.

So, let's pick up the iron axe-head out of the water, secure it back onto the handle, and go to work.

Action Items

1. What are some items that are within your control?
2. What are some things that are outside your control?
3. Are there things in your home you've been putting off fixing because you don't know how? Make a homeschool project day, and get those things done—or, if too involved, hire those jobs out.

Bible Verses

Write these out in the space given:

Isaiah 41:10

Romans 6:16

Overwhelmed

1 Corinthians 9:27

Chapter Five

Stress

Recently, I was overwhelmed to the point I was having anxiety attacks often. My cup was empty, yet I was still trying to pour from it. You can't pour from an empty cup: you can't give and give to your family, your church, your homeschool, even your husband if you have nothing to give.

Stress does that to a person. It can wear you out and make you physically ill. Being in a season of complete overwhelming stress can affect you in many ways: spiritually, physically, relationally, and in your homeschool. It does seem that if one thing happens, five more things follow.

If there is one thing that can quickly add to overwhelming feelings and thoughts, it's stress. The state of being constantly stressed out (often called being overwhelmed) is physiological in nature. Triangle-shaped organs at the top of your kidneys called adrenal glands make cortisol[2]. Cortisol is an important hormone that keeps inflammation down; manages how the body uses fats, proteins, and carbs; regulates blood pressure and sleep/wake schedule; and increases blood sugar. Adrenal glands are important for our health.

Overwhelmed

When stress enters the picture, the hypothalamus and pituitary gland send signals to the adrenal glands to increase the amount of cortisol to deal with the situation that's causing stress. That's what's called the "fight or flight response." This can be good in emergencies as it gives us a boost of adrenaline to deal with situations.

However, when our bodies are bombarded by overwhelming, *constant* stress, the adrenal glands go into hyperactive overdrive making cortisol. Too much cortisol can wreak havoc on a body, including creating anxiety and depression, trouble sleeping, headaches, memory and concentration issues, digestion

Overwhelmed

problems, weight gain—even heart disease. All those symptoms can create more cortisol just from the stress of having them.

Sound familiar? It does to me. The carousel of madness that can be my life is often just that—a constant circle of too much busyness, too much stress, too much drama, and often, I do it to myself. All that is reflected in how I'm doing physically. Stress begats stress and one of the culprits of that coupling is busyness.

Homeschoolers tend to want to "make up" for everything their child is "missing" in public or private schools, so they join multiple co-ops, sports teams, playdates, drama programs, music lessons. I know right now we're staring at tennis lessons twice a week, co-op once a week, and appointments besides, and somehow, by the grace of God, we need to fit academics into the week.

What that creates is a lifestyle of constant stress and on-the-go-ness: in a valiant effort to provide opportunities for our children, we wear ourselves (and them!) completely out. Our families are fatigued beyond our ability to describe it, and the issue goes far deeper than just chilling with the remote control and resting. We have to make *real change* in our *lives* to reduce stress and get our bodies in good operating order. It begins with slowing down and decreasing the stress in our lives.

The prophet Elijah knew about stress. After God had wrought a miracle, Elijah rounded up all the prophets of Baal and had them killed. The evil queen Jezebel issued a death warrant on Elijah's head, and, fearing for his life, Elijah ran.

> "Elijah was afraid and ran for his life. When he came to Beersheba in Judah, he left his servant there, while he himself went a day's journey into the wilderness. He came to a broom bush, sat down under it and prayed that he might die. "I have had enough, LORD," he said. "Take my life; I am no better than my ancestors." Then he lay down under the bush and

Overwhelmed

fell asleep. All at once an angel touched him and said, "Get up and eat." He looked around, and there by his head was some bread baked over hot coals, and a jar of water. He ate and drank and then lay down again.

The angel of the LORD came back a second time and touched him and said, "Get up and eat, for the journey is too much for you." So he got up and ate and drank. Strengthened by that food, he traveled forty days and forty nights until he reached Horeb, the mountain of God. There he went into a cave and spent the night," [1 Kings 19:3-9]

It took an angel of the Lord to cook him a meal, provide water, and tell him he needed real rest. Not the kind that can be had by watching television or going on a cruise, but the kind that is provided by Christ Himself. In the Bible, *broom trees* are often symbols of God's provision for rest, food, and water. Elijah was spiritually, physically, and emotionally exhausted and needed the rest that can only come from Jesus, as is stated in the Gospel of Matthew. "Come to me, all you who are weary and burdened, and I will give you rest," [Matthew 11:28]. No wonder then that Jesus said, "…I am the bread of life. Whoever comes to me will never go hungry, and whoever believes in me will never be thirsty," [John 6:35] and "For the Lamb at the center of the throne will be their shepherd; 'he will lead them to springs of living water.' 'And God will wipe away every tear from their eyes,'" [Revelation 7:17].

Jesus is the Living Water, the Bread of Life, and the One Who can provide Rest. It is not a coincidence that the angel provided Elijah with bread, water, and rest—He, like us, needed the rest that can only come from Jesus.

Homeschooling parents have so much on their plates: managing the home, caring for children and often their own parents, and homeschooling on top of everything else. It can be exhausting. If you add in a part-time job, remote working, or working from home

Overwhelmed

full-time, *plus* all of the above, you forget to take care of your own needs quickly. The cortisol avalanche hits, and your body reacts to stress by creating internal stress. This isn't good—we *must* take care of ourselves to take care of those Whom God has entrusted to us.

The apostle Paul was once shipwrecked with some very angry and frightened sailors, who had been tossed in the angry Adriatic Sea for an amazing fourteen days. When at last the boat crashed against rocks and was lost, not a single sailor was killed—but they were mentally and physically beat. "Just before dawn Paul urged them all to eat. "For

Overwhelmed

the last fourteen days," he said, "you have been in constant suspense and have gone without food—you haven't eaten anything. Now I urge you to take some food. You need it to survive. Not one of you will lose a single hair from his head." After he said this, he took some bread and gave thanks to God in front of them all. Then he broke it and began to eat. They were all encouraged and ate some food themselves," [Acts 27:33-36].

Often, when we are stressed, the last thing we think about is food for ourselves. Jesus knew that the throngs of people would not be receptive to hearing His preaching

Overwhelmed

with aching, hungry bellies – that's why He always fed them first. Moms and dads, please listen—I once thought I was dying from inflammatory arthritis, but it turned out to be incredibly low vitamin D levels. Once I got that straightened out, my energy increased, joints hurt a lot less, and I now can play with my daughter. Eat healthy meals, drink water, and work on your relationship with Christ. In that way, you can calm those overwhelmed nerves and tend to the family of which God has blessed you.

Action Items

1. Make a doctor's appointment for a physical if you haven't had one in a while, and check on any problem areas with your health.
2. Buy some quart mason jars, fill four with water, and place in the refrigerator overnight. Drink them throughout the day, and in no time you'll have had a gallon of water in a day.
3. Institute a set bedtime for the household, and stick to it, even yourself. Dim the lights two hours before, turn the television and other screens off, and read actual books— either individually or as a family. This will help wind people down and make for more effective sleep.

Bible Verses

Write these out in the space given:

1 Corinthians 6:19-20

Overwhelmed

Exodus 15:26

1 Timothy 4:8

Jeremiah 17:14

Deuteronomy 7:12-15

Chapter Six

Comparison

A homeschooling friend of mine has tea parties. She posts the sweetest images on social media—so relaxing that I wish I was in her homeschool. Not as a parent or anything, just as a person stopping by to read a book and drink hot tea out of a real teacup with a saucer.

It's lovely.

I wanted to do that with my daughter in our homeschool.

Overwhelmed

My daughter, as sweet as she is, loves all things dinosaurs and cats and her stable of imaginary friends. What I envisioned our homeschool being: peaceful, full of eagerness to learn, never arguing or fighting, has hardly ever come to fruition. Sure, there are days that are like that, but there are also many days in which I have to raise my voice for Laura to get on her schoolwork.

My homeschool will not look like your homeschool, and that is okay. It is when we *envy* someone else's homeschool to the point that we are so very unhappy in our own situations that strife occurs. Theodore Roosevelt once said, "Comparison is the thief of joy," and he was right. Comparison leads to being overwhelmed because no matter what you do, you will not be able to obtain the source of your envy. There's nothing wrong with wanting to improve things; the problem occurs when you obsess about others' homes, homeschool spaces, *children*...and not be content in what you have.

Paul wrote in Philippians 4:11-13 (ESV), "Not that I am speaking of being in need, for I have learned in whatever situation I am to be content. I know how to be brought low, and I know how to abound. In any and every circumstance, I have learned the secret of

Overwhelmed

facing plenty and hunger, abundance and need. I can do all things through him who strengthens me."

Some parents are blessed with homes large enough to have a dedicated homeschool space; some families utilize the dining room table. Personally, I've had both, using a past bedroom for a homeschool space. But I found we were still in the dining room and on the living room couch more than in the homeschool room. In our open concept house, it makes sense to do homeschool in the areas of the house in which we do life. We have to homeschool how it helps our family; you have to homeschool how it benefits your family.

In our homeschools and lives, we must put God at the center of it all, and base what we do in His will. Our children are but our's for a season, in which to grow them, mold them, and train them up for service to the Lord, in whatever way God leads them.

What is your focus?

Why do you homeschool? Is it to prevent your child from learning things in public schools that are counter to your beliefs? Is it because your special needs child wasn't being given the resources or time or patience to learn? Is it because you

Overwhelmed

were fed up with the state of the public school system?

Ultimately, the *why* of what we do should be to glorify God. All those reasons above are Part Bs to glorifying God. To minimize the overwhelming difficulty that can be homeschooling, we must focus in on comparing less (our homeschools versus the local public schools) and what God would have us do.

Galatians 1:10 states, "For am I now seeking the approval of man, or of God? Or am I trying to please man? If I were still trying to please man, I would not be a servant of Christ." Do we homeschool to

Overwhelmed

impress our friends who are homeschoolers and got us into this, or do we homeschool to please God?

Our homeschools should reflect who we are as families. For us, we homeschool because our daughter (who has chronic migraines, dyslexia, and ADHD) was getting further and further behind in public school, and we didn't like what we saw coming to our county's public school system, based on what we saw at the state level. Plus, when we started homeschooling, I was caring for my now-deceased mother, and homeschooling allowed me the freedom to do that and teach Laura about caregiving,

Overwhelmed

too. But none of that means one iota compared to this: we homeschool because we, as a couple and as a family, believe God led us to choose this lifestyle for our daughter. It allows us the freedom to *disciple* her in the Word of God and in the Christian faith, throughout all her studies and in life, too.

Someone once said to me, "Does Laura get up at 7 a.m. and start school at 8 like in public school?" Uhm…no. As a child who has migraines, she needs her sleep. I need my sleep! Plus, we're not replicating public school. We're not even doing school-at-home. *We homeschool*…that means that she

Overwhelmed

doesn't have to raise her hand if she needs to go to the bathroom or get a drink of water. It means we can do reading time on the comfy couch. It means we can watch YouTube videos to supplement our curriculum and, if we're not feeling well, we can watch documentaries and call it a school day.

It's when we try to compare and keep up with other homeschoolers, public or private schools, or other families – instead of following where God leads – that we become overwhelmed. James 3:16 states, "For where jealousy and selfish ambition exist, there will be disorder and every vile practice." Where jealousy (envy) is, there is disorder (overwhelmed), and "…God is not a God of disorder but of peace," [1 Corinthians 14:33a NIV]. So let's stop comparing our homeschools and families to others, and live the life in which God has called us.

Action Items

1. Discover and write down the *whys*: why do you homeschool?
2. Write down mission and vision statements for your homeschool, type them out, and frame and display it as reminders of why you do what you do.
3. Read the following Scripture verses about comparison, and ask God to reveal lessons in them for your particular situation.

Bible Verses

Write these out in the space given:

Overwhelmed

Galatians 6:4-5

2 Corinthians 10:12

1 Thessalonians 4:11-12

1 Corinthians 3:3

Overwhelmed

Romans 12:2

Chapter Seven

Alone

I think one of the most overwhelming situations to be in as a homeschooler is doing it alone. Whether you're a single parent, or being married but homeschooling without spousal support—either is excruciatingly difficult. Homeschooling without extended family support is tough, too.

We can gain some encouragement, though, from the story of Timothy in the Bible. In Acts 16:1, we read "Paul came to

Overwhelmed

Derbe and then to Lystra, where a disciple named Timothy lived, whose mother was Jewish and a believer but whose father was a Greek." Although Timothy's father was unnamed throughout Scripture, we know from 2 Timothy 1:5 that Timothy lived with his mother Eunice and his grandmother Lois.

We don't know a lot about Timothy's father, but we do know that because his mother was Jewish, Timothy needed to be circumcised eight days after birth. Being Greek and possibly a non-believer as his faith is never mentioned, or even possibly dead, Timothy's father didn't participate in

Overwhelmed

the Jewish ritual and therefore it wasn't done; in fact, Paul circumcised Timothy when he was older and even called him "my beloved child," [2 Timothy 1:2]. Regardless, Scripture omits Timothy's father from the record of faith, and often, what Scripture leaves out is often just as telling as what is left in. Timothy's father was not active in his spiritual life, for whatever reason. Timothy's father did not disciple his son in the Christian faith.

What is left in, though, is incredibly encouraging to parents homeschooling their children on their own without spousal support. Lois, the grandmother, had taught

Overwhelmed

her daughter Eunice about Jesus, and together, they raised Timothy up in the faith. Although Paul certainly had a hand in Timothy's upbringing in the faith, Paul is quick to underscore the importance that Lois and Eunice had in his life, saying, "I am reminded of your sincere faith, which first lived in your grandmother Lois and in your mother Eunice and, I am persuaded, now lives in you also," [2 Timothy 1:5].

Paul writes, that "…from infancy you have known the Holy Scriptures, which are able to make you wise for salvation through faith in Christ Jesus," [2 Timothy 3:15], showing that from infancy Eunice and Lois

Overwhelmed

were alone in Timothy's Christian education. It doesn't say *why* they were alone—perhaps Timothy's father was dead, or perhaps, he wasn't a believer.

Homeschooling families come in all shapes and sizes. There are families who have one child and those who have many; there are families who have both parents who are active in their children's lives and there are families who are headed up by one parent.

Single-parent homeschools have their own challenges, whether they're caused by death, divorce, or discord. Perhaps one parent is set upon homeschooling whereas

Overwhelmed

the other is so dead-set against it that he or she offers no help whatsoever. Or, the parent who is not active is around and a good parent, but all the homeschooling is left to the other one. Regardless of how one gets to Rome, you're in Rome nonetheless.

Eunice and Lois took it upon themselves to teach young Timothy the Scriptures, and therefore, about Jesus—leading him to such a faith that Paul used him on many missionary journeys and to pastor churches. Single parent homeschools will have good results, if children are given a firm foundation in the Word, lots of love, and consistency. Don't get discouraged, for God

Overwhelmed

can do the work if only we surrender to Him and give Him the glory. Ephesians 3:20-21 states, "Now to him who is able to do far more abundantly than all that we ask or think, according to the power at work within us, to him be glory in the church and in Christ Jesus throughout all generations, forever and ever. Amen."

If you're a single parent homeschool, don't give any ammunition to the absent party (or extended family) to give you grief about your homeschooling decision. Don't complain about the children not listening or that you can't find a certain curriculum—and defend your children during every

Overwhelmed

episode when unsupporting relatives or (groan) strangers want to quiz your children, especially when they don't quiz kids who are in public schools. There's no room for such behavior.

When I was a single mom, I clung to two different Scriptures: "A father to the fatherless, a defender of widows, is God in his holy dwelling. God sets the lonely in families," [Psalm 68:5-6a (NIV)]; and Isaiah 54:13 (ESV): "All your children shall be taught by the LORD, and great shall be the peace of your children." This brought me so much peace to know the Lord cares about my children's education.

Overwhelmed

The Lord God sees you. *He sees you.* Give your children and their education to the Lord, and—look at what Isaiah 54:13 stated: *"All your children shall be taught by the LORD, and great shall be the peace of your children."* He sees you as you struggle to manage your home and homeschool by yourself, and He will provide for you. Immerse yourself in the goodness of God's word, pray throughout the day to Jesus, tell your children of the goodness of God, and be led by the Holy Spirit to do what is right, holy, and peaceful for you and your children.

Overwhelmed

As for family members who are outright antagonistic towards *your* decision to homeschool *your* children, remind them of that: those babies are *your responsibility*, and you are accountable to no one but God Himself for them. Regarding a spouse who isn't helpful: prayerfully consider Christian counseling, especially if your spouse isn't towing the line with being the spiritual leader of the home, or not helping with household duties. After all: are you married, or do you have a roommate?

Regarding those with military spouses, as the mother-in-law of a sailor. Do your level best to teach your children when your

Overwhelmed

spouse is deployed, laying down consistent rules and expectations, including the kids helping with keeping the home (life skills!). Be sure to join military spouse groups for support and encouragement, especially military family homeschool groups or co-ops. But when your spouse is home, especially after deployment, let homeschool sit for a bit and just be a family. Enjoy that time. When you homeschool when your spouse is home, develop ideas on what your spouse can teach the children. Perhaps different life skills, or simply doing family reading—get him or her involved so they can see that homeschool is working and it's a viable option for your family.

A word of warning

If you are married, and homeschooling without help and indeed, with a lot of anger about homeschooling from your spouse, and your spouse is abusive to you and/or your children, *especially* if he or she is an unbeliever—*get out*. Go somewhere safe and leave. As a mom who was in an abusive marriage before, I can tell you this: I would be dead right now if I had not left. This type of situation goes beyond being overwhelmed; it's about safety and, often, life-or-death. Your children learn all they see; do you really want them to learn how to abuse their wife? Or have your daughter learn that she should tolerate abuse from her husband and stay "for the kids?"

Carrying the weight

Being overwhelmed with homeschooling and all that entails is one thing, but carrying the weight of it all without help, support, or encouragement is something else. You don't have to take it. If you are instructing your child biblically and sharing Jesus with him or her, that is more important than any negative talk from relatives.

If married, talk with your spouse. Ask for more help or interaction. Most of all, pray for your spouse. You are not your spouse's Holy Spirit—you can pray, but you

Overwhelmed

have to move out of the way to let God work. Don't try to force it.

If you're not married and a single parent, look for options to get your children involved with other kids, like youth group or Trail Life for boys and American Heritage Girls[3]. During the times when these groups meet, use that time to decompress, do a quick grocery store run by yourself, or just rest. During my daughter's American Heritage Girls' meetings, I waited on her in our church and wrote this book, while another homeschooling single mom organized her curriculum for the week and graded papers.

Overwhelmed

You see, though I am married, there are many times I feel like a single mom, due to my husband's paralysis. Yes, he works out of the home, but there are many days when he comes home that he's exhausted. Unrelenting nerve pain does that to you. Homeschooling and home management are all up to me, so I am very much doing it alone; it feels like resources are as scarce as my energy. A widow in the Old Testament faced a similar situation:

> "A certain woman of the wives of the sons of the prophets cried out to Elisha, saying, 'Your servant my husband is dead, and you know that your servant feared the LORD. And the creditor is

Overwhelmed

coming to take my two sons
to be his slaves.'

So Elisha said to her, 'What
shall I do for you? Tell me,
what do you have in the
house?' And she said, 'Your
maidservant has nothing in
the house but a jar of oil.'

Then he said, 'Go, borrow
vessels from everywhere,
from all your neighbors—
empty vessels; do not gather
just a few. And when you
have come in, you shall shut
the door behind you and your
sons; then pour it into all
those vessels, and set aside
the full ones.'

So she went from him and
shut the door behind her and
her sons, who brought the
vessels to her; and she
poured it out. Now it came to
pass, when the vessels were
full, that she said to her son,
'Bring me another vessel.'

Overwhelmed

> And he said to her, 'There
> is not another vessel.' So the
> oil ceased. Then she came
> and told the man of God. And
> he said, 'Go, sell the oil and
> pay your debt; and
> you and your sons live on the
> rest.' [2 Kings 4:1-7]

The Lord God sees your needs and can use your current resources to provide for you. God cares about single moms *and* single dads; God cares about parents who are married but for whatever reason, shoulders the bulk of the work. Elisha told the widow to go around to all her neighbors and borrow containers to put the oil in. Even though *she* knew how much oil was in the original jar, in faith she went to her neighbors and borrowed. The oil kept

Overwhelmed

coming until there wasn't another jar to be found, then the oil stopped. She had enough to provide food for her family and to sell the rest to dispose of the debt.

Even though I'm not a single mom now, my neighbors know the situation with my husband being paralyzed. They've helped us with car issues, mowing our grass, taking care of Laura during times of medical crisis, and other innumerable activities. The Lord has blessed me with neighbors, just like the widow. What if the widow's neighbors had laughed at her, shutting the door in her face, and refusing to give her a container? God

Overwhelmed

used the neighbors' generosity to help the widow.

In faith, the widow took the containers and poured the oil she already had, and kept pouring…and kept pouring…God can keep your resources going too, if you have faith in Him. What could have been a disastrous, overwhelming crisis, God turned into a miracle and a time of praise.

Action Items

1. What resources do you have that you can ask the Lord to use, to provide for you and to glorify Him? Pray about them.
2. If you're a single parent, research groups and activities for your children to gain some time for yourself.

Overwhelmed

3. Pray about talking with your neighbors and telling them your situation, or build a tribe of help through your church family.
4. Talk with your church about starting a single parent ministry with play dates, oil changes, discipleship classes, home repairs, etc.

Bible Verses

Write these out in the space given:

Psalm 37:4

1 Corinthians 13:4-8

Matthew 28:20

Overwhelmed

Luke 11:11-12

Philippians 3:8-16

Overwhelmed

Chapter Eight

Caregiving

One of the blessings of homeschooling is the ability to teach children who are medically fragile and need to be at home, for their safety and health. Another blessing of homeschooling is the freedom to teach children how to take care of elderly or disabled relatives.

The issue is that blending homeschooling and caregiving can be a recipe for becoming overwhelmed with the amount of work these entail separately, not

Overwhelmed

to mention combined. Before my mother died, I was going to her senior apartment at least three times a week, with my daughter. We would often do homeschool in the morning then save the afternoons for Mom, unless she had a morning doctors appointment. If that happened, I packed up worksheets and books and we did homeschool in waiting rooms and listened to audio books in the car.

Was this tough? Yes. Did Laura learn? Oh, yes. She not only learned academics but also learned how to test blood sugar, do blood pressure checks, and how to be a

Overwhelmed

caregiver. She learned empathy and how to serve.

With my husband's paralysis and doing things with and for my autistic son, caregiving is a part of life in our homeschool. It's a part of life in many homeschools across the country. The things that children can learn in caregiving will be with them for their entire lives as they marry and have kids of their own, or even enter the medical field.

It's not without being overwhelming, though. Making expectations clear and keeping communications open about doctor visits are crucial. I remember asking my

Overwhelmed

Mom to please schedule any doctor visits for afternoons, if at all possible. That helped me have the mornings free for academics. Going to a four-day homeschool week helped, too, because Fridays were Mom's day to go grocery shopping, get her hair done, and other errands. Now, Fridays are designated for Sam and his errands.

On the now-rare days that Laura presents with a migraine, we know homeschool will not happen that day. She will take her meds and stay in her darkened room with a damp wash cloth on her eyes. If we forced the issue, she wouldn't learn anything because of the pain. The point of homeschooling is

Overwhelmed

the flexibility to do life together as a family, and you just cannot compartmentalize things like this is school, this is caregiving, this is grocery shopping. All of it is homeschooling, even on days when Laura is learning how to care for herself with a migraine—that is homeschooling.

When we use caregiving as an integral and necessary part of homeschool life, we put feet to our faith. Jesus said, "Whatever you did for one of the least of these brothers of Mine, you did it for Me," [Matthew 25:40]. When we help others by bringing a casserole to an overwhelmed homeschool mom, or someone who's had a death in the

Overwhelmed

family, or serving with our church family at community events, we're serving Jesus. I cannot think of a better way to learn than to serve Jesus.

When Mom or Dad is the one who's ill

As someone who has chronic illnesses, there are often days that I am feeling too sick to instruct Laura on subtracting unlike fractions. Can I get a witness? There are days I wake up with a migraine, or just not feeling well. On days like this, public school teachers can call in a substitute; homeschool parents have to get creative as they homeschool and parent from bed or the couch.

Overwhelmed

I've been known to make a "sick day" packet with review-type material that my child can do on the floor beside me if she needs guidance. This packet contains a fill-in multiplication chart (once a child starts learning the multiplication tables, constant review is vital to continued memorization), spelling words she's had in the past for review, a simple grammar workbook purchased at a teacher supply store, and other worksheets aimed at reviewing past lessons.

I've also turned on the television for us to watch documentaries on topics we've been studying in Bible, history, or science.

Overwhelmed

You can often have a full homeschool day just doing these things—from the comfort of your own couch. You can also have your child read to you, or to him- or herself. When all else fails, there is always reading to do.

If there's a looming hospital visit in your future for either mom or dad, or if a serious disease has reared its ugly head in your family, it's imperative you keep track of what lessons are to be done with your kids, in case an adult caregiver (such as a grandparent or other responsible adult) needs to step into the role of homeschooler and caregiver.

Overwhelmed

During times of extended illness, when my mother-in-love would visit and take over homeschooling Laura while I attended to either my sick mother or my husband, I would make daily packets for her. These packets would include a daily lesson plan, any worksheets and instructions, and would stay on top of any books Laura would use that day. Communication in times of caregiving is a critical part of family life, including homeschooling.

My mother was diagnosed with lung cancer on September 14; two weeks after diagnosis, she died at our home in the early morning hours of October 1. I was an

Overwhelmed

emotional wreck, as I dealt with the funeral home, the church for her service, family members, and my own fragile emotions. During the entire month of October, as we worked on cleaning out her apartment and settling estate things, and crying daily, homeschool was the last thing on my mind. Laura, who considered her Memaw to be her best friend, was in no state to work on decimals or world history or nouns.

So we took the month of October off.

And that was okay.

Homeschool gives you the freedom to deal with life—or death. In that month,

Overwhelmed

Laura learned immeasurable lessons about Heaven, salvation, grief, dealing with overwhelming emotions, and other big-ticket items that aren't in textbooks. We needed that month off academics to deal with life. Caregiving is part of that.

In an online homeschool group I'm in, I read a message from a homeschooling dad whose wife had just died. Their little girl cried daily in her public school classroom, and was terrified that her dad was going to die and leave her, too. So the dad, who worked from home, decided to homeschool her. He was overwhelmed from the emotional trauma of daily life, and was

Overwhelmed

seeking advice on what to do with homeschool. In that situation, just love each other. Read a lot. Color. Give it time. The academics can wait; the healing cannot.

In caregiving and homeschooling, one of the most important things we can do is to rest. Jesus said in Matthew 11:27 (NIV), "Come to me, all you who are weary and burdened, and I will give you rest." When we come to Jesus, exhausted and torn apart emotionally, He comforts us—through His Word, through other believers, through music, and through physical rest.

Action Items

1. Create a "sick day" packet for each child, that includes a weeks-worth of review-type worksheets. Put them in manila folders with the child's name on them and keep where you can easily get to them or tell someone where they are.
2. Create a playlist of appropriate videos in YouTube for sick days, based on what is currently being studied about in your homeschool
3. Communicate with anyone you care for about days and times you are not available.

Bible Verses

Write these out in the space given:

Matthew 11:29-30

Overwhelmed

Psalm 62:1

Psalm 4:8

Psalm 23:1-2

Psalm 91:1-2

Overwhelmed

Chapter Nine

Home Management

One of the hardest parts about homeschooling is managing all the stuff on the home front: cleaning, cooking, maintenance, laundry. *Laundry*.

Ironically, as a home maker, wife, and mom, one of the most convicting and humbling passages in Scripture is Proverbs 31:10-31—

> "An excellent wife who can find? She is far more precious than jewels. The heart of her husband

Overwhelmed

trusts in her, and he will have
no lack of gain.
She does him good, and not
harm,
all the days of her life.
She seeks wool and flax, and
works with willing hands.
She is like the ships of the
merchant; she brings her food
from afar.
She rises while it is yet
night and provides food for
her household and portions
for her maidens.
She considers a field and
buys it; with the fruit of her
hands she plants a vineyard.
She dresses herself with
strength
and makes her arms strong.
She perceives that her
merchandise is profitable.
Her lamp does not go out at
night.
She puts her hands to the
distaff,
and her hands hold the
spindle.
She opens her hand to the
poor
and reaches out her hands

Overwhelmed

to the needy.
She is not afraid of snow for
her household, for all her
household are clothed
in scarlet.
She makes bed coverings for
herself; her clothing is fine
linen and purple.
Her husband is known in the
gates
when he sits among the
elders of the land.
She makes linen garments
and sells them; she delivers
sashes to the merchant.
Strength and dignity are her
clothing, and she laughs at
the time to come.
She opens her mouth with
wisdom, and the teaching of
kindness is on her tongue.
She looks well to the ways of
her household and does not
eat the bread of idleness.
Her children rise up and call
her blessed; her husband also,
and he praises her:
"Many women have
done excellently, but you
surpass them all."
Charm is deceitful, and

Overwhelmed

> beauty is vain, but a woman who fears the LORD is to be praised.
> Give her of the fruit of her hands,
> and let her works praise her in the gates."

This passage is certainly intimidating. Managing a home properly—cleaning, laundry, maintenance, yard work, decluttering—is nearly a full-time job. Add in homeschooling and working a bit for pay, and there's no time to sleep! It's certainly overwhelming.

The thing about the Proverbs 31 woman is this: we know she had children and she obviously taught them, as she "opens her mouth with wisdom, and the teaching of

Overwhelmed

kindness is on her tongue." In biblical times, children were expected to help with the household: doing chores, farming, weaving, taking care of livestock. Perhaps we need to take a lesson from this industrious lady and include home management life skills into our homeschools.

As I see it, I'm not rearing a little girl. I'm rearing a girl who will be a woman one day, with her own home, own family, own children. Her own vehicle, taxes, and checking account. She needs to know how to do things before she flies out of the nest. If I was homeschooling boys, they would need to know how to take care of a home, too,

Overwhelmed

just like my daughter will know how to change the oil and tires on a car (I'm planning on asking my youngest son to teach her, as my husband cannot).

Besides the future-driven aspects of learning how to manage a home, teaching life skills has a very practical application. It helps parents to involve all who live in the home to take care of the home. Children of all ages, except babies, can do chores—and should be expected to.

Even toddlers can have a clean-up time. Preschoolers can learn how to sort laundry (socks and underwear in this pile, shirts and pants in that pile). Older children can learn

Overwhelmed

how to unload the dishwasher, reload it, sweep or vacuum, even mow the grass. The point is, everyone of age who live in the home can contribute to managing the home, and learn valuable life skills in the process.

Yet, the home can still (and more than not, usually is) be a source of overwhelming frustration. Our expectations of what it's like to be at home full-time need to be lowered—it's awfully hard to clean, keep kids alive, homeschool, keep pets alive, help the husband, and cook healthy or semi-healthy meals, day in and day out. Something has to give.

Overwhelmed

Many years ago, I had the thought of wanting a really nice dining room area in which to entertain friends and family. After getting frustrated for months, I came to the realization that we don't entertain that often, maybe twice a year. It was causing my family a lot of unwarranted stress, this desire to have a magazine-worthy dining room space and homeschool in it. What are the purposes behind your living spaces? Answer this question and you'll soon design and implement family-friendly areas that complement your lifestyle, not create conflict within it.

Meals

Regarding meals, the most energy I have is in the morning, so while Laura is working on spelling, I get out my slow cooker and put something on for dinner. This frees up my early evening to either prepare other dishes, clean up something, or write.

There are many tools one can utilize to help with meal prep. Allowing your children in the kitchen during this time will help with additional hands to prepare food (learning another life skill!) and have quality family time in the process.

My daughter prefers to snack more than eat actual meals…it's a source of great irritation. I make sure that there is always fresh fruit like apples, bananas, celery sticks, and carrots available, and tell her to go for those before the chips and crackers. It's an uphill battle, of which I win some skirmishes and lose others. Unfortunately, she has my love of carbs so there's that. I have found, though, that if I don't buy it and bring it in the house, she (and I) will snack on the healthy things we have in the house.

Project Days

In my home, I love project days. These Saturdays get everyone helping on a list of projects. It could be repairing a plumbing leak, or mulching the flower beds out front,

Overwhelmed

or deep cleaning the living room. We've installed water filters under the kitchen sink, a new porch light, even did small car repairs like putting in a new headlight. The beauty of project days is that many maintenance-type items get checked off the list, and important life skills get taught to the children, including the concept of taking care of your property. Even people who live in apartments can have project days, such as deep-cleaning rooms, rearranging furniture, putting shelving units together, or sorting through clothes to keep, repair, and donate. You don't have to own your home to take care of it—or to teach your children valuable skills in the process. Homeschool isn't regulated to the dining table, or Monday through Friday. Often the lessons kids learn best are the ones they don't even realize are part of "homeschool."

Home blessing

The Proverbs 31 lady was remarkable in how much she accomplished, but she couldn't do all she did without the Lord's help. One of the most valuable activities you can do is to go through your home, as a family, and pray to God to bless each room with His peace and presence.

Dedicating our very homes to the Lord and living out our faith in them will teach our children to lean on Him. Actively

Overwhelmed

reading the Scriptures together as a family will do that more than any amount of chores. Sometimes we get caught up in how our homes look than the attitudes that prevail inside them.

If we look at Proverbs 31:10-31 objectively and not as a to-do list of epic proportions, we can see that managing our homes, businesses, and leading our families are activities that can honor God and help make our lives easier, not harder. Like many families, I have had a great deal of clutter—in my home, my schedule, my emotions. The Proverbs 31 woman had no time or energy for clutter; if it wasn't useful to

Overwhelmed

body, mind, or soul, or to her purse, she didn't pursue it. Looking at our calendars, shelves, cabinets, attics, and garages with objectivity, and disposing of things that either don't bring God glory, or take time away from our families, could be an avenue of prayer and action.

We tend to fill up empty spaces in our lives with knick-knacks or time fillers. Scrolling social media is one that fills time and not necessarily in a good way. As someone who blogs and uses social media in my business, it's part and parcel of what I do, but I've been guilty of watching cat videos or getting involved in social media

Overwhelmed

drama at bedtime to the point it's hard to wind down. Just writing that is convicting—the Proverbs 31 woman wouldn't be doing that, she'd be either turning the dishwasher on to run during the night, or reading her Bible at bedtime. She'd sleep, and get up well-rested and ready to attack her day.

As you think about your home and lifestyle, I want to encourage you: whatever action you decide to take, do it with a lot of prayer and input from your family. Get them involved. Managing a home is a great deal easier when everyone is involved—and God is at the forefront.

Action Items

1. Institute a daily, out-loud, Scripture reading time at a time that works best for your family
2. Write out a meal plan for the upcoming week, and go grocery shopping for it. Buy healthy snacks your family will eat.
3. Look at your house with fresh eyes. How are rooms being utilized—for your family, or to entertain people who aren't there? Can you repurpose rooms to serve greater needs, and if so, how?

Bible Verses

Write these out in the space given:

Psalm 84:3

Psalm 127:4

Overwhelmed

Proverbs 24:3

Psalm 26:8

Chapter Ten

Expectations

One of the biggest causes of being overwhelmed in our lives, and indeed our homeschools, are expectations—either too high, or too low. Too high, and you risk making your homeschool a source of stress for you and your children; too low, and your kids will become bored and frustrated with their homeschool.

When we first started homeschooling, I tried to recreate what I thought kindergarten looked like, based on my boys'

Overwhelmed

kindergartens in public school. I had a dedicated homeschool space, with desks for her and myself. Bright, colorful pictures adorned the walls, and unique things from nature (seashells, rocks, pine cones, etc) were on a table to be inspected. That was all well and good, but my expectations were of public school or doing school-at-home settings. It was pretty stressful for both of us.

Now, with a few years of homeschooling under my belt, we're no longer trying to recreate a wheel that's not working. We're *homeschooling*, based on our family's needs and the academic and life skill needs of our

Overwhelmed

daughter. We homeschool based on God's leading, and making it Christ-centric instead of us-centric. Core subjects like science and history have a definite biblical basis, and we study the Bible together. We pray together. We talk about Jesus often in homeschool. When we get out of the way and surrender to God's will, amazing things will happen.

Jonah had high expectations. He was sent by God to the godless city of Ninevah, and didn't want to go, because he believed the people in that city were not worthy of God's favor, forgiveness, or redemption. Yet, he *knew* God would forgive them—that's why he bolted to Tarshish. "And he

Overwhelmed

prayed to the LORD and said, 'O LORD, is not this what I said when I was yet in my country? *That is why I made haste to flee to Tarshish; for I knew that you are a gracious God and merciful, slow to anger and abounding in steadfast love, and relenting from disaster,*'" [Jonah 4:2, emphasis mine].

Jonah's expectations of what *should* happen to Ninevah did not correlate to God's will—the people cried out to God and He saved them, which disappointed Jonah immensely. In our homeschools, we will not get disappointed if we align our expectations with God's will for our lives and the lives of our family members.

Overwhelmed

Judas Iscariot left the somber upper room after he had his feet washed by Jesus, the night of the Last Supper, and visited the high priests to deliver Jesus into their hands.

Why the timing on this? Why not leave before, or wait a few days for the high priests to go after Jesus themselves? The answer is in what happened just a couple of days and, indeed, hours before.

On Sunday, Jesus rode into Jerusalem on a donkey—a victor's welcoming, palm branches and all. He accepted this welcoming and did not stop the shouting of praises. Monday, He drove the money-

Overwhelmed

changers from the temple with authority and railed against the Pharisees and Sanhedrin.

Jesus, then, delivered a series of powerful, no-holds-barred parables on Tuesday. For someone like Judas Iscariot, who was the holder of the ministry's treasury, Jesus' words must have made his jaw drop as he realized Jesus was not here for an earthly kingdom.

I can only imagine what Judas thought when the Pharisees sought to trap Jesus with His words. Maybe now, Judas may have thought – maybe now Jesus will tell them He's come to lay waste to the Romans. But when the Pharisees asked, "Tell us then,

Overwhelmed

what is your opinion? Is it right to pay the imperial tax to Caesar or not?" [Matthew 22:17].

Then Jesus, knowing they were trying to trap Him, opened His precious mouth with the powerful words, "You hypocrites, why are you trying to trap me? Show me the coin used for paying the tax." They brought him a denarius, and he asked them, "Whose image is this? And whose inscription?"

"Caesar's," they replied.

Then he said to them, "So give back to Caesar what is Caesar's, and to God what is God's." [Matthew 22:18b-21].

Overwhelmed

Maybe, Judas may have thought, maybe he hadn't heard right. Surely Judas' savior was this man Jesus. Where was the profit in giving back to Caesar and giving back to God? When the disciples followed Him away from the temple and to the Mount of Olives, Judas heard Jesus' words again, this time detailing for His most loyal followers what the end times would entail. "Then you will be handed over to be persecuted and put to death, and you will be hated by all nations because of me," Jesus said in Matthew 24:9.

For someone like Judas, who only heard what he wanted to hear, Jesus' words about the servants with the masters' gold must

Overwhelmed

have bee-lined straight for his ears. "'So take the bag of gold from him and give it to the one who has ten bags. For whoever has will be given more, and they will have an abundance. Whoever does not have, even what they have will be taken from them. And throw that worthless servant outside, into the darkness, where there will be weeping and gnashing of teeth,'" [Matthew 26:28-30].

To add injury to insult, in Judas' depraved mind, there's Jesus, talking with important people around the dinner table – when in walks this…. *woman…*

Overwhelmed

"A woman came to him with an alabaster jar of very expensive perfume, which she poured on his head as he was reclining at the table. When the disciples saw this, they were indignant. "Why this waste?" they asked. "This perfume could have been sold at a high price and the money given to the poor."

Aware of this, Jesus said to them, "Why are you bothering this woman? She has done a beautiful thing to me. The poor you will always have with you, but you will not always have me. When she poured this perfume on my body, she did it to prepare me for burial. Truly I tell you, wherever this

Overwhelmed

gospel is preached throughout the world, what she has done will also be told, in memory of her," [Matthew 26:7-13].

You see, Judas had his hand in the moneybag all along. John wrote, "He did not say this because he cared about the poor but because he was a thief; as keeper of the money bag, he used to help himself to what was put into it," [John 12:6]. He didn't care about the poor; he cared about making a profit for himself.

That very night, after Jesus rebuked him, he made a clandestine visit to see the high priests, who had been looking for a way to grab Jesus. Matthew 26 states, "Then one of

Overwhelmed

the Twelve—the one called Judas Iscariot—went to the chief priests and asked, "What are you willing to give me if I deliver him over to you?" So they counted out for him thirty pieces of silver. From then on Judas watched for an opportunity to hand him over," [14-16].

Why 30 pieces of silver? That's an awfully exact amount. Listen: in the study of Scripture, there are lessons in such specifics. Looking back in the Old Testament, Exodus 21:32, what is the price of a slave? "If the bull gores a male or female slave, the owner must pay thirty shekels of silver to the

Overwhelmed

master of the slave, and the bull is to be stoned to death."

Thirty shekels of silver.

Jesus was sold off by someone who believed whole-heartily in the prosperity gospel for *thirty pieces of silver*. The price of a slave.

Judas initiated the betrayal – the high priests did not approach him. Judas was so close to Christ – called one of the Twelve throughout the Gospels – but he still did not get it[4].

You see, Judas *expected* Jesus to be an earthly messiah—one to throw off the yoke

Overwhelmed

of Roman oppression. When he realized Jesus's kingdom was of a spiritual nature (oh, how he misunderstood! A relationship with Jesus is about the mind, body, and soul—all of it!), he dove for the first opportunity to throw Jesus to the wolves.

Judas' expectations and actions were all part of God's plan. Jesus knew Judas would betray Him, knew all along that there was a devil among the twelve disciples.

We can have high expectations for our lives and for our homeschools, but if they don't dovetail with God's plan, we're chasing our tails. Conversely, if we have

Overwhelmed

too-low expectations, we don't ask enough of our children.

My daughter has dyslexia. I bought her a reading guide, a colored piece of plastic she uses to read books and papers, line-by-line. It's a tool to help her with reading. Do I allow her to read on a lower level because it would be easier? No. The only way to grow is to expand your horizons and try to do something more difficult than you think you can do.

Realistic expectations

When it comes to keeping a clean, uncluttered house (I can just hear a laugh track here!), *and* homeschool, having

Overwhelmed

realistic expectations is crucial to keeping yourself sane. It's about priorities and keeping the things that are non-negotiables and easing up on things that, in the big picture, don't matter. It's important to keep the dining table cleaned off to do homeschool in the morning; is it really important to clean the entire house just to make a social media reel?

The Big Picture

The big picture is this: we all get overwhelmed to some degree. It all depends on who we are. My autistic son gets overwhelmed by straw wrappers and trash; my daughter's room is a veritable homage to

Overwhelmed

dumpster diving (we're working on it). The important thing is to keep Jesus as the focus of all you do, in homeschool and life, because what you do in His will, to build His kingdom, has eternal consequences.

To decrease getting overwhelmed, make changes in your life to minimize the opportunities to become overwhelmed. I know this is simplified, but sweet parent, take note of this: "**For I consider that the sufferings of this present time are not worth comparing with the glory that is to be revealed to us**," [Romans 8:18].

Be at peace, sweet parent. Love on your children and play with them. Read the Bible

Overwhelmed

as a family. May the peace of Jesus be with you as you homeschool in the will of our Lord.

Action Items

1. Write out your academic expectations for each of your children. In talking with them, how can each child make those expectations into achievable goals?
2. Are there things in your home that are non-negotiable chores? Have some project days and knock those out.
3. Is clutter driving you crazy? Have a massive decluttering project day and haul stuff off (either donate, trash, give away, or sell).

Bible Verses

Write these out in the space given:

Overwhelmed

Hebrews 13:8

Psalm 46:1

Philippians 4:6-7

James 1:2-4

Endnotes

Chapter 3
1. https://findwords.info/term/mephibosheth

Chapter 5
2. "What is Cortisol?" Medically Reviewed by Arefa Cassoobhoy, MD, MPH on December 13, 2020. https://www.webmd.com/a-to-z-guides/what-is-cortisol

Chapter 7
3. Trail Life: https://www.traillifeusa.com/

   American Heritage Girls: https://americanheritagegirls.org/

Chapter 10
4. "The Price of a Slave; The Price of a Savior," by Terrie Bentley McKee, April 11, 2017, http://www.nearyouraltar.com/blog/the-price-of-a-slave-the-price-of-a-savior

About the Author

Terrie Bentley McKee is a follower of Jesus Christ, wife to Greg, mom, homeschooler, author, blogger, and podcaster. She has four children in a blended family, plus two bonus children by marriages. In addition to blogging at Homeschooling1Child.com and its complementary podcast, she teaches adult Sunday School at her church.

Overwhelmed

www.ingramcontent.com/pod-product-compliance
Lightning Source LLC
Chambersburg PA
CBHW031249290426
44109CB00012B/507